LOVES LUMINESCENCE

**A POETIC EXPLORATION OF TIME
HOPE & HUMAN EXISTENCE**

AMY CECILIA GRAINGER

LOVES LUMINESCENCE

AMY CECILIA GRAINGER

©2025 Amy Cecilia Grainger
All rights reserved.

First published 2025

No part of this publication may be reproduced, stored in a retrieval system, or transmitted in any form or by any means—electronic, mechanical, photocopying, recording, or otherwise—without prior written permission of the author.

Disclaimer:
This work reflects the author's philosophical inquiry and lived experience. It is intended for personal reflection and creative exploration only and does not constitute professional advice or instruction. Readers remain solely responsible for their own interpretations and actions.

Author:
Amy Cecilia Grainger

Published by
Souls of Ones Feet

Graphic Design & Cover:
Ged L. M. Buick
ISBN: 978-1-0683830-3-8
:

We are love. We are love -
We are dancing through a space
Where we evolve in the energy
We eloquently place grace

"When transformation aligns with timelessness
There resides a space to breathe
Love and hope bring harmony
Patience aids to heal"

THE EVER EXPANDING NOW

BEGINNING
In the beginning there was dust, molecules and magic – a dance so extravagantly tragic, a collision, a composure, of a new world that grows older – the beginning – kept expanding – and now – times is not withstanding.

BRIDGE
Welcome to this poetic exploration of time, space, human existence and hope. Feel this book as a gift, a journey of from my heart to yours.

Release any expectations.

Allow yourself to travel – to unravel – to evolve as you explore!

BEACON
Allow the words of these explorations to illuminate the avenues of your time.

Feel love, feel peace, feel hope in your heart.

Be time.

BACK TO A BEGINNING
When we evolve time disintegrates - we uncover a space often reserved or overlooked - time does not end.

It infinitely- begins again.

CONTENT

THE EVER-EXPANDING NOW..7
MESSAGE FROM THE AUTHOR 11
INSPIRATION SURROUNDS US 14
THE LIGHT OF LOVE...19

FLOW ONE 26
FLOW TWO 30
FLOW THREE...34
FLOW FOUR...38
FLOW FIVE 42
FLOW SIX...46

FLOW SEVEN...50
FLOW EIGHT..54
FLOW NINE..58
FLOW TEN..62
FLOW ELEVEN 66
FLOW TWELVE...68

POETIC EXTENSION INTRO..............................75
LOVE ECHOES..78
MORE IN THIS SERIES..81
INVITATION TO EXPLORE FURTHER..............84

Love is not only a physical phenomenon,
it is a language of hope, a vibration held in time.

MESSAGE FROM THE AUTHOR

HOW DOES IT FEEL TO BE HUMAN?

Welcome to this poetic series, which offers an alternative way to examine a philosophy of hope - a philosophy I refer to as the Souls of One's Feet.

This journey began long before I could grasp the depth of its significance. Now, after much turbulence and many transitions, I bring my philosophy to life. Like all human explorations this is going to be turbulent maybe a little uncomfortable.

Souls of One's Feet is about what carries us when nothing else does - a lifelong invitation to hold hope; a vibration that has been at the heart of my musings for over two decades. For me an exploration on what it means to be human.

After much deliberation, observation and exploration, I have concluded that for me, being human is a journey of hope. Over time, I have mused in meanders mapping a poetic series that serve as a bridge to my philosophy. This bridge begins with The Timekeeper... although you may read any of my works in an order you choose...In remembrance that we all arrive in our own space - in time.

Throughout our human journey, we navigate endless avenues of emotion. We seek a middle ground - a harmonious balance - we never quite land in this space, not until we leave this earthly place.

What exactly are we searching for?

Why are we here?

What does it mean to be human?

There exists an empty space I refer to as the 'middle-way' . This is the space, where we pause. The space we feel between our humans experience. These pauses form, what I describe as sequences; sequences I map through my time.

In my observations, hope expands mostly in the sequences of joy. Rarely is it remarked upon in the quieter, more subtle sequences of discomfort. As human beings we dance through light and dark. Through the ebb and flow we call life, we are the dance of existence in time.

Each human experiences time that challenges them, a happening that changes the structure of reality. A loss, a trauma, a profound shift in how it feels to be human. These moments create ripples in frequencies that move through us. If they feel uncomfortable we may avoid-dance. We are always - dancing.

The purpose of these poetic explorations is to illuminate the sequences of hope and formulate a bridge to my life's work a philosophy that comes from my heart. To experience my musings in the hope that is intended I invite you to feel time and space in a way that may appear unusual, uncomfortable, or even uncertain. In this discomfort time expands. Uncertainty deepens our awareness of time, in these spaces we may examine layers of our existence through a lens of hope.

love

INSPIRATION SURROUNDS US

Love is the original light — the glow before the dawn, the warmth beneath the skin of all things, including time. It is not confined to hearts or hands or names; it spills from the sky, hums in the ocean, and blooms in the silence. When inspiration sparks in our hearts loves presence is near - in the space between worlds hope memos echoes.

WE ARE THE LIGHT

Every emotion, even sorrow, is lit from within by something sacred, a spark that is constant. The ache of longing, the thrill of connection, the stillness of solitude — all are illuminated by the embers of hope that flow through the chambers in your chest. We are walking constellations, unknowingly radiant, each carrying a piece of loves spark. Love's luminescence does not burn; it revives, it connects and in its most abundant it creates through a vibration of hope.

These poems that follow are not answers, maybe lanterns. They offer no map, only moments — brief illuminations that remind us: we are never separate from the love than binds everything that created us and everything that divides - everything between you and I - every pulse - every shadow - love softly guiding us to remember who we are.

Read along with me on my poetry channel.
Let's journey together through the verses, allowing the words to resonate and unfold.

www.soulsofonesfeet.bandcamp.com

THE LIGHT OF LOVE

SOULS OF ONES FEET
A PHILOSOPHY OF HOPE

Loves Luminescence is an invitation to witness the quiet and vibrant dance between love and light, between hope and time. How do we hold love as human beings if not through the radiant vibration of hope which offers us tender reflections that echo from the heart. I refer to these chambers as houses.

The light of love's illuminates the darkest corners of our being, spiking the shadows that sit dormat and hidden. The shadows would not exist without the light we call love. Nor the place we hold hope. For the shadows are echoes from a space where time once was - and is no longer. Spaces in time we hold on to - How do we hold onto the energy arrived through - the vibrations that now sqew - time present and time new.

Each poem is a exploration on how love moves through us, like light reflecting off water, changing its shape with each moment, yet always part of the same infinite source - a source we map across time, a source that holds us anchored - I refer to this as a vibration of hope. It reminds me that love is not merely something we give or receive, but something we embody, something we become.

How do we feel love in its warmest embrace,
if not with a dash of hope...

FLOW ONE

There is a vibrancy to feeling
A human unrevealing
A middleway
      A meader
An energetic extravaganza

We are human energy
           and love is energy to
It flows through the avenues - expanding in arenas of time
When joy and grace and eloquence bring faith
When the disharmony decreases
The energy as we know it - merges and time ceases

Love bellows - like a gentle woven craft
Gracefully, patiently
A hopeful ventured path
           No looking back......

Here we are navigating the then - through the now

Energy

    Energy
A loving luminescence
When gifted with a gentle presence

We are only energy
Energy is love too-
       It flows through me as it flows through you

There is a core at the heart of humanity
A space that is unmechanical
          and it resonates when we beat
In the steps that we take - through the Souls of One's Feet

FLOW TWO

This is your vibration
           Your melody - your flow
Love cascaded in avenues

A bellow

       A bellow

Hold your heart - feel it beat
A bellow in acceptance
     not a bellow in defeat
You in your best energy
  Through the love you hold and show
Meander
     Gently meander
A luminescent glow

Nature unfolds with eloquence
A breath that lights our world
The love that falls between
A graceful - dance - a swirl

I will say this repeatedly
It will echo through a known
That love anchors through a timeless flow
A middle-way we wend
In experiences, ancestral deficiencies
A time and a whence not when

Love bellows in the distance
Through every avenue
The grands, the elders
The ancient sacred few

An illuminated conundrum
A trail of time through space

A bellow

      A bellow

Love held in grace

FLOW THREE

Energy - Energy bellows with belonging
Have you opened your heart yet to the love that is for-longing
Step out of those spaces
        entangled interlaces
Step out of those spaces
              Where hope cant breathe nor be
Step out of those spaces
      Feel the echo in the beat
Beat
    Beat
            Though the Soul of On's Feet
Through a vibration in accordance
With how our time should be
The ripples of energy form through love...
You see...
      There are light waves
             illuminated light waves
Cast is energy that's bound
To land through a harmonious
Peaceful
     Hopeful sound
A bellow
    A whisper in the breeze
Love landing in subtle degrees

We are only energy and energy is love too

When we harmonise

       When we synchronise

When we hold our space

      When we attune

We hold an open chamber
        For our energy to breathe - we bloom
Where the mechanical rhythm fades
Far into the distance where - love it cascades

We are only energy and energy is love to
It beats through me as it beats through you

In this hopeful day - through our energy
In our love - a bellowing vibration
An accordance through contemplation
A vibration

      A luminescent flow
Love
   Love

        Love

A gentle bellow

There is a core at the heart of humanity
A space that is unmechanical
and it resonates when we beat
In the steps that we take - through the Souls of One's Feet

FLOW FOUR

Love - kind - sweet love
Shines brightly
      even amid the dark
It illuminates
        It illuminates
A gentle stroll - a - walk
A Meander - to arrive from here   to   there

No rush - only patience
Purpose through loves flare

There is energy, held in avenues
Energy held in revenues
Energy seeps through our structure
Where love holds space in time
As we meander through the meadows

Breathe - now align

There is movement
There is motion
There is space - there is devotion
Yet the rhythm is elusive
Universally divine
A purpose - through a heartbeat
Love's luminessence flows through time

We are love
    We are love
We are dancing through a space
Where we evolve in the energy
We eloquently place grace

Vibrations flow through the galaxies
Vast velocities
Bellows
    Bellows

Seeping through fears to hide
The echoes

    The bellows

Love - only - illuminates life's ride

The avenues your heart goes
      As it meanders through the halls
To ascend through alchemation
An illuminated transfiguration
      An awakening
An enlightenment
Call it what you will
The purpose in your heart space
Love illuminates hope

    Time stand still

FLOW FIVE

There is a space that pulsates
As the flow that finds the waters
A fall, a cascade
North to east
       South to west
There is a purpose to your compass
It is held within your chest

Your heart's intrinsic footwork
Gentle steps - balanced
Through a universal embark
A meander through a meadow
A climb upon a mountain
To swim beneath intrinsic time
A heart within a fountain

A compass
       A guide
Weathering times stride
Eloquently through the avenues
Of the space in time we hide

Love it does illuminate
When we hold time through our heart space
A gentle pace
       Navigation
Magnetisation
Illuminated
Enlightened
Awaken
       Awaken

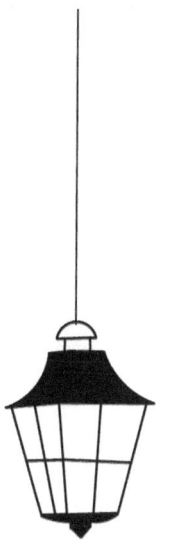

FLOW SIX

There are these facets
fixtures and fittings
Ridges
    Ridges
Rectangles and stitches
Patterns
Luminous patterns
Between the spaces
The unoccupied labels
Forms of human fables

Time passes

     Time Passes

Feel through the chambers - centred in your core
Love illuminate the avenues like it never has before

The luminescence
        The luminescence

          The flow

Love bellows
        As it echoes
The fear gently glides
We breathe - we feel
As time - it subsides

There is this flow, that falls through a middleway
  - love held within a frequency
A pulse in passions delinquency

Love luminates these avenues
Through the rhythm to your time
As you feel within your human core

Your structure

    Most divine

There is this space that pulsates
As the flow that finds the waters
A fall, a cascade
North to east - south to west -
There is a purpose to your compass
It is held within your chest

FLOW SEVEN

There is this woven war
Where love attempts to land
Yet we humans continues to pushback
        through time we reprimand

The avenues most illuminent
The avenues we pursue
The avenues most hopeful
        In the core of me and you
Hope is

Love is what we are born to
A luminescent light
To breathe into existence
Our time as it takes flight

We create
    We build
We nurture
From the beginning we meet an end
Illuminating abundance
A gentle - lifelong friend

You see
Time is frequency
        - love is an energies thats bound
To be held within a treasured space
An element quite profound

A joyful extraction

                A peaceful contraction

That resides within the chambers of your soul

Beyond the mechanical

Where love and fear fold

A gentle meander

        A stroll

FLOW EIGHT

The universe is showing
The perceptual rays on parade
We travel
     Where time in space is made
A perpetual glorious shade

Love within its comfort - its illuminating walls
As the heart begins to expand
Embody - as time calls

The luminescent light waves
The love beyond all time
As the mechanical disintegrates
This world of yours and mine

You see there is no hierarchy - when it comes to love
A pure frequency - eloquent - interwove

Through the tapestry
The time
     The trajectory most divine
That this journey we all embark
Where the lightness meets the dark
Guides us to a central space
A location held in time
        A love in luminescence
A space one should enshrine

Yet in this modern world we question
We demand a physical expression
An object, a barrel - to barter
To blame the navigation we charter

It is we, that choose the patterns
We that choose the trends
Through deliverance
            In acceptance
When we acknowledge where love wends

FLOW NINE

Consciously we unravel
Through the climatic calculations
As love illuminates in sacred formulations

Our world is our grandest puzzle
We are a sequence held in tow
As we attempt to unravel our knowing
In all that being human does show

The universe is guiding
The perceptual rays on parade
We dance as we adventure
Time as time does fade

We illuminate
We attenuate
Through passion and spark
Hope in its most graceful
As eloquence lights the dark

We grant gentle understanding
Where we hold love with hope
As they drift away in the cosmos
Where the fears tend to lope

The universe is healing
As the perceptual rays parade
Time in hope allurance
Through the gift which love has braved
Illuminating the hallways
An eloquent luminescent parade

Your heart meanders through these halls
To ascend through alchemation

Where Love calls

           Fear falls

Consciously we unravel
Through the climatic calculations
As love illuminates in sacred formulations

FLOW TEN

Have you ever sat and pondered
Where time in space it flows
Through the vibrations
Only loves luminescence knows

Chambers
Chastisement
A critical retirement

    A pocket

A parallel peace

    A patience not quite perfect

  A dance

A luminescent dance
You see, to find the light we embark the dark
Yet the purpose most uncertain
As we contemplate to feel
The chambers
      Only chambers
Our passion most surreal

So we tip toe, and we tally
We balance as we dally
Through the doorways
      Through the hallways
In the chambers of our heart
To meet a luminescent love
As light
    It streams the dark

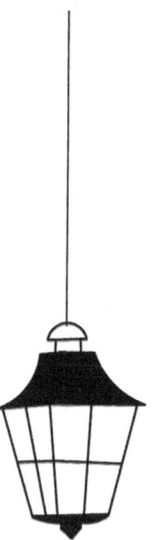

FLOW ELEVEN

Traditions deem antiquity
Tradition fall in time
To present us with an order
To unravel thee divine

There is this bellow
That echoes
Through the light waves held in love
A sacred understanding
    A sanctuary through a core
That expands the physical
Like we have never known before

There is a electromagnetic connection
More pure than humans have known
That pulsates through the passages
Of a gentle persuasion we call home

Love

Comfort

Compassion

A patient grace

A dance most illuminant

Where one's energy does meet with faith

FLOW TWELVE

We arrive once again at a beginning
Where loves luminescence shines most bright
As we dance within the joys of space
A vision with delight

The corridors the chambers
The contours and exchanges
We emerge
Through the light waves we diverse
We immerse
Through the chemistry

In love
   Patient - graceful love

There are these flows that fall through a middleway
Where love illuminates the world
It is here where hope meanders
At a gentle pace

         A swirl
A spiral in divine deliveration
An extreme form of overwhelmation
Through the light waves
Through the love
Through compassion which we choose
In the pathways and the avenues
Where one's heart becomes the muse
Love -
   Gentle
Patient
   Persistent
Love

Bellows through the hallways of time
Echoing through existence
As we dance our way -
           - through this world of yours and mine

So we tip toe, and we tally
We balance as we dally
The doorways, through the hallways
In the chambers of our heart
To meet a luminescent love
As light it streams the dark

**GRATITUDE & LOVE
LIVE HERE**

LOVE ECHOES

POETIC EXTENSION

As we reach the final verse of this poetic journey, I invite you to pause and listen to the quiet echo of love that reverberates through the spaces we inhabit as human beings - in remembrance that Love in its many forms, is a constant thread entwined into the avenues of time through a vibration of hope - a melody that pulses softly through the chambers of our human chest.

The vibrations that bring us discomfort lead us to digress a dance in fear, I refer to this as a tip toeing exploration to arrive at the house of I am here. In this space I feel love echo.

All of my poetic explorations have an extension, musing left over and made into - something extended - in this space they formulate an echo of love that lands through hope.

As you journey through these words, I ask you to consider how love, in all its forms, echoes in your life. Allow these words to stir the stillness within you as you connect to the eternal rhythm of love that pulses through your heart centre.

The echo of love never truly fades it returns again and again, its essence carried forward on a vibration of hope, ever-present, ever-resonating, quietly reverberating through the space your time lives.

LOVE ECHOES

Love echoes in the halls,
                where time falls

        Like, Our, Virtuous, Emotions
Space beckons
                Time recalls

An internal emotional conflict
        ushers
                    through the avenues we wend
Bound by time before and after
        In the spaces we transcend

The brightness
    The being
The clarity for seeing
The light waves
        The light waves - the love
The heart of hope is breathing

Love falls in a middleway
It illuminates the senses
It battles with our fears
It cascades our hopes defences

                Like, Our, Virtuous, Emotions
        Space beckons. Fear falls
A friendship
        A lover
An ancestor, a brother
All initiated from the beginning of a father and a mother
Labels - mere labels
That aid to guide the way

Through the love - in the light waves
    luminescence that decays
Only in the physical
      The meta is divine
Listen through your heart space

SHINE - SHINE - SHINE -

At the heart of being human
Through our structure and our core
Love illuminates the halls
Like it never has before
Through the beats in the bellows
Earthly human echoes
When we examine time in a pulse
When we hold space
When we gift - patience with grace
We allocate time for the echoes
For the gentle drift of the bellows
To merge through hope to love

At the heart of being human
    through our structure and our core
Love illuminates the halls, like it never has before
Where the after began in the forecourt
      In the space between
Love echoes in a way that only time has seen

The dance it continues...
Through a space of silent sound
An undercurrent, a thunderstorm
A legacy. - A heart
A human heart
Carries the journey of one,
      through pathways of many
Sound - Silent Sound
Ambiguous - profound
Love bellows - where time echoes
Round and Round

OTHER WORKS BY AMY CECILIA GRAINGER

A Philosophy of Hope

The Space Time Lives In
Emerging Through Time and Space

Selected Poetry Collections
The Timekeeper
Houses of Hope
Transforming Trees
Chemistry

CONTINUING THE INQUIRY

HOW DOES IT FEEL TO BE HUMAN?

Thank you for spending time within these poems.

Loves luminescence forms part of a wider body of work exploring time, hope, and human existence through both poetry and philosophy. While these poems approach experience through image and rhythm, the philosophical works examine the same questions through sustained inquiry.

If the reflections within this collection resonate with you, the exploration continues in:

The Space Time Lives In
Book I of A Philosophy of Hope

With Love
Amy S

www.ingramcontent.com/pod-product-compliance
Lightning Source LLC
Chambersburg PA
CBHW030455010526
44118CB00011B/946